# Mr Punch

## Steve Byron

### developed in collaboration with Joana Geronimo

T0179816

*methuen* | drama

LONDON • NEW YORK • OXFORD • NEW DELHI • SYDNEY

METHUEN DRAMA
Bloomsbury Publishing Plc
50 Bedford Square, London, WC1B 3DP, UK
1385 Broadway, New York, NY 10018, USA
29 Earlsfort Terrace, Dublin 2, Ireland

BLOOMSBURY, METHUEN DRAMA and the Methuen
Drama logo are trademarks of Bloomsbury Publishing Plc

First published in Great Britain 2023

A catalogue record for this book is available from the British Library.

A catalog record for this book is available from the Library of Congress.

ISBN: PB: 978-1-3504-5193-3
ePDF: 978-1-3504-5194-0
eBook: 978-1-3504-5195-7

Series: Modern Plays

Typeset by Mark Heslington Ltd, Scarborough, North Yorkshire

To find out more about our authors and books visit
www.bloomsbury.com and sign up for our newsletters.

Alphabetti Theatre in association with The Worriers present

# Mr Punch

## Written by Steve Byron

### Developed in collaboration with Joana Geronimo

**Mr Punch** was first performed at Alphabetti Theatre,
on Tuesday 12 September 2023.

**MR PUNCH**

Written by Steve Byron
Developed in collaboration with Joana Geronimo
Co-created in association with The Worriers

**Cast**

Norman | **Steve Byron**
Ruth | **Joana Geronimo**

**Creative & Production Team**

Director | **Paula Penman**
Writers | **Steve Byron with Joana Geronimo**
Stage Manager | **Chris Foley**
Costume and Set Designer | **Ali Pritchard**
Puppet Designer and Builder | **Molly Barrett**
Assistant Set Builder | **Daniel McMillan**
Lighting Designers | **Chris Foley and Ali Pritchard**
Sound Designers | **Gina Ruffin and Paula Penman**
Photographer and Videographer | **Benjamin Michael Smith**
Producer | **Gina Ruffin**

**From Alphabetti Theatre**

Artistic and Executive Director | **Ali Pritchard**
Venue Producer | **Esther Fearn**
General Manager | **Sam Johnson**
Executive Assistant | **Clare Overton**
General Supervisor | **Lizzy Jakeman**
Technical Coordinator | **Chris Foley**
Community Engagement Coordinator | **Audrey Cook**
Marketing Coordinator | **Scott Jeffery**
Associate Producers | **Gina Ruffin and Chloe Stott**
Associate Literary Manager | **Ben Dickenson**
General Assistants | **Rosie Bowden, Sarah Bulmer, Nicole Freeman, Willow Gregson, Eve Hitchens, Siobhan McAuley, Damien Reay, Owen Saunders, Andrea Scrimshaw, Reka Szalkai, Kieren Wadforth, Miles Warburton, Carl Wylie,**
Access Consultants | **Richard Boggie, David Oliver and Ruth Patterson**
Theatre Dog | **Rex**

## STEVE BYRON (he/him)
(Writer and Performer)

**Steve Byron** is an actor, writer and theatre practitioner with over thirty years of experience working in the North East. Recent acting credits include *When The Boat Comes In* (Customs House); *Sunset Over Tantobie* (Gala Durham); *A Viking Christmas, Whale of a Time* (Alphabetti Theatre) and *Sleeping Beauty* (Gala Durham). His writing credits include *Reiver: Tales from the Borders*, and for Alphabetti Theatre: *Bacon Knees and Sausage Fingers*, *Floorboards*, *Rocket Girl, Sucking Eggs* and *Tree*.

## JOANA GERONIMO (she/her)
(Writer and Performer)

**Joana Geronimo** is an Angolan actor, writer and theatre practitioner based in the North East. Recent acting credits include: *From Home to Newcastle* (Live Theatre); *The Space Between Us* (Open Clasp); *HERE* (Curious Monkey); *The White Card* (Northern Stage); *OUT, OUT!* (Alphabetti Theatre). Recent writing credits include *OUT, OUT!* (Alphabetti Theatre).

## PAULA PENMAN (she/her)
(Director)

**Paula Penman** has twenty-three years' experience working as an actor, director and theatre maker, most notably for regional and national tours of solo shows *Donna Disco* (Live Theatre, Winner of Wimbledon Theatre's *Best of the Fringe Award*) and *Brown Bird* (Bush Theatre).

Other acting credits include: *The Remarkable Robin Armstrong's Extraordinary Christmas Adventure* (Queens Hall, Hexham, Alnwick Playhouse); *The Snow Queen*, *Get Santa!*, *The Little Detective Agency*, *The Goblin Who Saved Christmas*, *The Hoppings* (Northern Stage); *Pause* (*The Stage's* top picks for 2021); *Three Shorts*, *Wrong Place Wrong Time*, *Bricks and Mortar*, *Christmas Carol* (Alphabetti Theatre); *Woven Bones* (shortlisted for *Performance of The Year Living North 2019*, Cap-a-Pie); *Stand 'n' Tan* (Open Clasp); *The Christmas Tree* (Gala Theatre, Durham); *Landslide* (PP Productions); *Finding Away (*Chilli Studios*)*; *Rat Boy*, *A Man in a Dress Talking About Football* (Luke Barnes, Live Theatre); *Emmerdale* (ITV).

Directing credits include: *The Gingerbread Man* (Triple Treat in association with Northern Stage); *Manifesto For a New City* (Project A Theatre Royal Newcastle); *Then Leap* (commissioned by and premiered at The Lowry); *Landslide* (PP Productions); *No.9*, *Whale of a Time*, *Listen Up!*, *Wilfred* (Alphabetti Theatre); *40 Kola Comedy Rolla* (Alphabetti Theatre, NE Comedy Hothouse); *County Lines* (Kendal Brewery Arts); *Space: A Herstory* (Curious Arts); *Chained Reaction, Networking: Your Voice North East, 10 Minutes to...* (Live Theatre); *Stupid R&D* (Northern Stage).

Paula is an ongoing Associate Artist with Theatre Royal Newcastle's training programme Project A and Associate Artist with Alphabetti Theatre. Her participatory work has led to collaborations with National Theatre and the RSC and in 2009 she was awarded the Channel 4 Just For Laughs Best Actress Award for short film *Car Trouble*.

## CHRIS FOLEY (he/him)
(Stage Manager)

**Chris Foley** has worked in theatres across the North East for over ten years. He began as an actor moving into facilitation but finally found himself working behind the scenes, in stage management, operating sound and lights as well as being a production assistant. His work has taken him from Newcastle Theatre Royal to Sadler's Wells and the Edinburgh Fringe to the Houses of Parliament. Working for Alphabetti Theatre has given Chris the platform to hone his technical skills, and the exciting challenge that comes with making high quality work with a smaller budget than other theatres in the region.

## GINA RUFFIN (she/her)
(Producer)

**Gina Ruffin** recently made roots in the North East after studying under the tutelage of Jim Cartwright and producing various theatre shows across Manchester's fringe scene.

She's passionate about producing work from authentic regional voices and making it available to all audiences, which matches the ethos of Alphabetti. For Alphabetti she has produced: *Sugar Baby*, *More Blacks*, *More Dogs, More Irish*, *Soapbox Racer* and *Chop Dissolve Burn*; and co-produced *Person Spec* and *Raven.*

## ALI PRITCHARD (he/him)
(Artistic/Executive Director)

**Ali Pritchard** founded Alphabetti Theatre in 2012 at the age of 22, making him one of the UK's youngest artistic directors running a venue. He has a degree in Drama and Scriptwriting from Northumbria University, and a Higher Diploma in Contemporary Vocals from The Academy of Contemporary Music. Ali is a visiting lecturer at a number of higher educational organisations across the North East, and in 2013 was awarded 'Best Postgraduate Lecturer' following a year-long graduate fellowship at Northumbria University.

Under Ali's leadership, Alphabetti have become a crucial part of the arts ecology in the region.

Ali has been involved in every Alphabetti Theatre production. His directing credits include: *Teeth In Eggcups*, *Three Shorts*, *The Frights*, *The Rooms*, *Bacon Knees & Sausage Fingers*, *Trolley Boy, Walter, Present, Opolis,* and *Song of the Goblins*.

His producing and writing credits include: *How Did I Get to This Point?*, *How Did We Get to This Point?*, *Present*, *Love From*, *Opolis*, and children's book *Keeping Time*, all for Alphabetti Theatre.

Ali was named as one of the Rising Stars of the UK theatre industry in The Stage 100 2023.


## ESTHER FEARN (she/her)
(Venue Producer)

Esther trained in Early Modern literature before working on new writing theatre with Alphabetti. Beginning as a volunteer in 2015, she has been working as Alphabetti's Venue Producer since 2019, and is passionate about championing underrepresented stories from North East artists.

Producing credits for Alphabetti include: *Three Shorts*, *Rocket Girl*, *Listen In*, *AWARE*, *Sucking Eggs*, *Pause*, *Tree*, *Mr Incredible*, *All White Everything But Me*, and *hang* as producer and assistant director.

Esther holds a Masters degree in English Literature, 1500–1900, and has produced playscripts for Alphabetti productions *Three Shorts*, *Tree*, *Chop Dissolve Burn* (with WANCs); and *All White Everything But Me*.

## SAM JOHNSON (he/him)
(General Manager)

From a young age Sam has been involved in Theatre and the Arts. After many years grafting in hospitality, alongside running a theatre company, he jumped at the chance to bring these two worlds together. Sam has been following Alphabetti's progress over the last ten years, so was really excited to join the team. He is responsible for running the day-to-day operations of Alphabetti, be that the bar, working on the website or booking events and rehearsal rooms.

## CLARE OVERTON (she/her)
(Executive Assistant)

Twenty years ago, Clare ran away to the Edinburgh Fringe Festival for the summer which is where her love of theatre began. She then spent the majority of her career working in finance and admin at Live Theatre, Newcastle before joining Alphabetti Theatre as Executive Assistant in 2022. Clare loves working at Alphabetti Theatre with the brilliant staff team and seeing fantastic artists making great work makes going to work every day a joy. In her spare time Clare volunteers as a Brownie Leader and enjoys her allotment when the weather is good, but will often be found baking cakes in the depths of winter.

## LIZZY JAKEMAN (she/her)
(General Supervisor)

Creative adjacent, beer-loving gal. Find her pouring pints with a smile in the beautiful Betti. She doesn't have theatre credits, but she does have a Masters in Film and a love for all things yellow. Known to match her mug to her outfit.

## AUDREY COOK (they/them)
(Community Engagement Coordinator)

Audrey Cook is a theatre maker and community arts practitioner from Teesside and has been working as Alphabetti's Community Engagement Coordinator since 2022. After graduating with a degree in European Contemporary Theatre from Rose Bruford College in 2020, they have been working professionally in the arts and culture sector since 2021, running regional community arts projects, and making theatre and live performance for queer, North East audiences. They have been supported by ARC Stockton, Alphabetti Theatre, Curious Arts, and many others.

## SCOTT JEFFERY (he/him)
(Marketing Coordinator)

A graduate of journalism, Scott has worked in marketing and communications for the past decade. Despite several forays into amateur theatre during his school and college years, his involvement today is largely centred around promoting shows as Alphabetti Theatre's in-house marketing coordinator.

## CHLOE STOTT (she/her)
(Associate Producer)

Chloe moved from the North West in order to expand her knowledge and experience of arts venues, after studying BA Theatre and Performance at the University of Leeds. She is ticket office manager at Dance City and, in Alphabetti's opinion, one of the most exciting freelance producers in the North East.

Chloe has worked with Alphabetti on a freelance basis since 2015, producing *Bacon Knees & Sausage Fingers*, *Trolley Boy*, *Christmas Cabaret*, *The Rooms*, *The Frights*, and *Tiny Fragments of Beautiful Light* to name but a few.

## BEN DICKENSON (he/him)
(Associate Literary Manager)

Ben has been passionate about arts, culture and social change since a taste of theatre transformed his life as a teenager. Becoming a culture convert he trained at Rose Bruford College, received a Masters in Film and Television from Westminster University, and studied for PhD at Goldsmiths College.

His career has encompassed writing for stage and screen, filmmaking, journalism, managing supported housing and youth citizenship programmes, numerous community arts projects, teaching film, and running services for disadvantaged children and young people. He has also written two critically acclaimed books, and produced a popular regional breakfast radio show.

As Executive Producer for City of Dreams, Ben led a ten year mission for Newcastle Gateshead Cultural Venues, making Tyneside the 'best place to be young' by engaging everyone under 25 in cultural activity. He is currently Chief Executive Director for Theatre Hullabaloo, and has worked with Alphabetti on a freelance basis since 2014, currently leading up Alphabetti's Arts Council England funded Just Write scheme.

**With thanks to our access consultants Richard Boggie, David Oliver and Ruth Patterson, and to our Board of Trustees: Jon Farthing, Hamish Carter, Christina Berriman Dawson, Jo Hodson, Jacqui Kell and Ruth Patterson.**

*'Not just an essential part of the region's theatre ecology...but the UK. Long may it continue.'* **British Theatre Guide**

**Alphabetti Theatre is an award-winning, artist-led performance space in Newcastle upon Tyne. We believe that great art should be for everyone, regardless of financial situation, and work to create great socioeconomically accessible theatre by, with and for our community.**

**We are the city's smallest producing house, making a big impact.**

Alphabetti was created to fulfil the need for a fringe venue in the North East, a place for early career artists to experiment, evolve and be inspired. It is a community-driven space, dedicated to enabling access to theatre, whether as a creative or an audience member. Through its lauded Pay What You Feel ticketing, artist development programmes, and homegrown talent, it's working to ensure the continued enjoyment and development of the performing arts in the region.

Since 2013, it has commissioned over 100 publicly funded projects, and provided support, guidance and opportunities for hundreds more creatives. Its new writing work has prompted discussion and praise from the theatre bar to the Houses of Parliament, and reflects the stories, people and issues of importance to its community. In 2023, Alphabetti was named Fringe Theatre of the Year 2023 at The Stage Awards, the first venue outside of London to win this award.

It recently celebrated its tenth birthday, and looks forward to the next.

🐦 Alphabetti

📷 alphabetti_theatre

📘 AlphabettiTheatre

## SUPPORT ALPHABETTI THEATRE

**Like what we do? Put your money where your mouth is! If you can. If you can't, please keep shouting about us.**

Alphabetti Theatre is an award-winning independent 80-seat theatre in Newcastle upon Tyne. We believe great art should be for everyone, regardless of financial situation. We are a space to experiment, evolve and discover excellence, for artist, audience and participants. Annually we average 300 performances, supporting 1,250 artist and welcoming 12,000 audience members.

We were built out of necessity by artists and the local community, and we need your support to continue develop the North East's performing arts ecology and better the lives of the people we come into contact with.

You can make a one-off donation via text:

Text 10BETTI to 70470 to donate £10

Text 20BETTI to 70470 to donate £20

To opt out of marketing text [CODE]NOINFO
Texts cost the donation amount plus one standard message.

We'd like to say a huge thank you to our current individual supporters:

Tom Greest          Tracey Sinclair
Mark Hanford        Conall Bolton
Neil Hayden         Lorna Cowen
Kate Parkins        Joe Hufton
John Appleton       Clare Overton
Elain Kernahan      Kate Denby
David Byrne         Jacqui Lovell
Rosie Bowden

Why not become a regular giver? Your monthly donation will keep the doors open and the lights on, allowing us to continue the work we do.

To find out more, visit our website:
www.alphabettitheatre.co.uk/support-us

# Mr Punch

## Characters

**Norman**, *an English man in his later years*
**Ruth**, *a woman from the world in her younger years*

## Voices

*Voices on the streets*
**Mary** *from downstairs*

## Setting

*All action takes place a small shitty bedsit.*

# Act One

## Norman

*A darkened bedsit. Light comes from a flashing light outside and behind the cracks in the door giving any detail. We can hear thumping music in the distance and voices shouting on the street.*

*We hear distant footsteps climbing stairs followed by a loud thump of something heavy being carried. The footsteps get louder yet slower indicating that whoever is climbing the stairs is beginning to struggle. This goes on for some time, until they stop on the other side of the door. We hear heavy breathing and coughing followed by the sound of keys falling to the floor.*

**Norman**   Arseholes.

*Sound of a struggle to bend down and pick them up.*

*Sound of keys going into the lock in the door, followed by them falling to the floor again.*

**Norman** *screams out in frustration.*

Fucking fuck.

*Sound of keys going into the lock of the door.*

FUCK.

*Sound of keys in the lock of the door.*

Come on, you fucker.

*Sound of a kick to the door.*

Open up you . . . cu . . . ome on.

*Sound of keys in the lock and kicking to the door.* **Norman** *is almost sobbing.*

Hold on droopy, you can do it.

*Sound of keys in the lock.*

**Norman** *begins to sing to distract.*

*'Song'*

*The sound of keys in the lock.*

Wait, wait, wait!!!

*Sound of a key finally turning in the lock.*

*The door is opened and we see the silhouette of a man stood next to a huge suitcase. He is holding a carrier bag. He is stood in a puddle of his own urine.*

**Norman** *is a middle aged washed out goth with a red nose.*

Arseholes.

**Norman** *reaches round to find the light switch. Lights on revealing a small and very badly kept bedsit. A bed and table to the left, a kitchenette table and chair to the right and two armchairs facing a television with a small table sat centre. Doors to the left and right lead to a bathroom and a bedroom.*

*Enter* **Norman** *dressed in a dark suit and coat. He drags the massive suitcase, but it gets stuck. He pulls it into the room, loses his balance pulling it onto him and falling to the floor.*

Fuck.

**Norman** *picks himself up, removes his coat and, picking up the case, throws it onto the table sending what was on it flying. He places the carrier bag on the table.* **Norman** *looks down at his wet trousers.*

Not on, droopy. We were nearly there. Every time you do this to me.

**Norman** *walks towards the door to the right, undoing his trousers as he goes.* **Norman** *exits.*

*We hear the sound of a water running followed by the clatter of a drunken man trying to remove his trousers.* **Norman** *falls with a loud clatter and the breaking of glass.*

Arseholes.

*Enter* **Norman** *wearing a towel around his waist, his hand is bleeding. He crosses to the kitchen cupboards. He begins opening and slamming the cupboards and drawers.*

A fucking break here?

**Norman** *gives up looking. He picks up a dirty tea towel and runs it under the kitchen tap. He then goes to the carrier bag and takes out a massive bottle of cheap and nasty cider. He tries to open it with great difficulty and pain with the bleeding hand. Finally opened he takes a large swig then pours some over his hand.* **Norman** *returns to the kitchen sink and wraps the now wet towel around his bleeding hand.* **Norman** *goes to the window.*

*Voices of abuse and laughter to* **Norman** *from the street below.*

Fuck off.

**Norman** *takes the bottle and a glass and sits in the chair.*

**Norman** *sighs.*

*The sound of someone slowly climbing the stairs and stopping at the door. There is a knock.* **Norman** *sits in silence. There is another knock.* **Norman** *looks strained. Another knock.* **Norman** *emits a loud and aggressive fart.*

Nice one, chatty arse.

**Mary**   Is everything alright, Norman?

**Norman** *looks round in his chair to face the door.*

**Norman**   Fine, Mary.

**Mary**   It's just I heard all the commotion outside and thought it might be those kids again.

**Norman**   Just me.

**Mary**   Floor's all wet.

**Norman**   What?

**Mary**   Floor's all wet, out here.

**Norman**    Out there? Floor's not mine out there, no man's land out there.

**Mary**    Well, it's very wet, someone could slip.

**Norman**    Pissing it down out there. Took a while to get the door open, would have run off my coat.

**Margaret**    Need a stronger bulb out here.

**Norman**    What?

**Mary**    Need a stronger bulb, you could slip.

**Norman**    Wanna push?

**Mary**    Been anywhere nice?

**Norman**    Funeral.

**Mary**    Nobody serious I hope.

**Norman**    No, just my dad.

*Long silence.* **Norman** *downs his glass and pours another.*

**Mary**    Was it sudden or?

**Norman**    No. He's always been my dad.

**Norman** *erupts into laughter for what seems an age. Once he has finally calmed down.*

**Mary**    Sorry for your loss, Norman.

**Norman**    Not a great loss really.

**Mary**    Anything I can do? I mean, when our Carol died. I was lost for months.

**Norman**    I'm not lost, well not yet.

**Mary**    So, if you need anything, Norman.

**Norman**    I will.

**Mary**    What?

**Norman**    Give you a shout.

**Mary**    Why?

**Norman**    If I need anything. I'll give you a shout.

**Mary**    I'll leave you in peace then.

**Norman**    Already in it.

**Mary**    Should get a mop on that rain, smells like cats' piss.

**Norman** *again breaks into hysterical laughter and laughs until he no longer sees what he is laughing at. He goes to the table and pours himself another large glass. He downs it in one. He pours himself another.*

**Norman** *reaches into his jacket pocket and pulls out his phone. He finds the number in the menu and pushes the dial button.*

**Norman**    Hoggy, Hoggy, Hoggy.

Hoggy, Hoggy, Hoggy.

Hoggy.

Hoggy.

Hoggy, Hoggy, Hoggy.

Hello, mate. Just me. Giz a shout, me dad's dead.

Cheers.

**Norman** *re-dials.*

Hello?

It's me.

Me.

Me.

Norman.

Norman.

**Norman** *begins to sing down the phone karaoke style. It's a duet so misses out the other lines.*

That's right.

We won a bottle of wine.

That's right.

Shared it in park.

Not all we shared though, was it.

Aye.

Aye.

Aye, sorry about that.

I've still got the stains.

Aye, when that old fella walked past with his dog.

**Norman** *laughs.*

Anyway.

You gave me your number.

Said to give you a call.

So I have.

So?

Right.

Really?

You didn't tell me that?

Kids?

Just wondered . . .

Just thought you . . .

Just thought.

My dad's dead.

Yeah, I know.

Couple of weeks ago.

It is.

I don't know.

I don't know.

I don't know.

He was in a home.

I don't know, so are you coming over then?

Oh right.

Is she?

Right.

Is she?

Is she?

Could she not look after them.

Right.

Right.

**Norman** *breathes a deep sigh.*

**Norman** *begins to sing the song again, it is soon apparent the other end has hung up.*

Give my love to your wife.

**Norman** *sits for a second.*

Wank?

**Norman** *picks up the remote control and searches through the channels. He watches for a bit, we hear various theme tunes* (Antiques Roadshow) *looks down, then sighs.*

Not tonight droopy.

**Norman** *picks up the bottle and pours another glass.*

You will always love me, won't you, my darling.

**Norman** *downs the drink like a disgusting kiss. He looks over to the table and sees the suitcase. He stares at it for some time.*

What are you fucking looking at?

You can just stay there and shut the fuck up.

This is my fucking house, I'll drink what I want.

You can't tell me what to do.

(*Under his breath.*) Not anymore.

Why don't you have a drink?

**Norman** *picks up the bottle and walks across to the case.*

I insist. Have one on me.

**Norman** *pours drink over the suitcase.*

Cheers.

**Norman** *looks at the bottle.*

All gone now, greedy.

**Norman** *reaches into the carrier bag and pulls out another bottle.*

Ta-da!!! Plenty more where that came from, we can have a proper send off. Just Daddy and his little Norman.

**Norman** *goes to the stereo. He goes through his CDs looking for something.*

**Norman** *places a CD into the player and plays something.*

**Norman** *begins to dance.*

Have a dance?

*He picks up the case and swings it around, it flies from his hand into the kitchen area where it does damage.*

**Norman**    Now look what you've fucking done. Give you a drink and you wreck the fucking place.

**Norman** *picks up the case and throws it onto the table. He sits catching his breath.*

**Norman** *drinks and stares at the suitcase on the table.*

Let's have a look at you then.

**Norman** *goes to open it and sees it's locked.*

Locked? Key?

**Norman** *looks and sees it's a combination lock.*

Combination.

Only you.

What is it then? A birthday?

**Norman** *sits racking his brains then jumps to his feet.*

I've got all the dates written down in a book so tough titty biscuits to you.

**Norman** *begins to pull the bedsit apart trying to find the book he is looking for, running from room to room. We hear a crash and* **Norman** *screaming in pain. He hobbles back into the room carrying the book.*

Right, let's have a look.

**Norman** *tries a series of combinations, with no success. Finally he slams the book down on the floor.*

Arseholes. Bet you're fucking loving this.

**Norman** *pours himself another drink and sits stewing.*

You know what, fuck you. Get in the fucking cupboard.

**Norman** *picks up the large case and drags it to a small cupboard in the wall, as he opens the door an ironing board and boxes fall into the room.* **Norman** *struggles to get them and the suitcase back in but finally manages it.*

And you can fucking stay there until you learn how to behave with some manners. Coming into my home, drinking my drink, smashing the place up?

**Norman** *slams the cupboard door.*

(*In a* **Mr Punch** *voice.*) That's the way we do it.

**Norman** *slams the door again.*

That's the way to do it.

**Norman** *slams the door again.*

*There is a knock at the door.* **Norman** *opens the cupboard door to check.*

*There is another knock at the door.*

Could you fuck off, please. I'm in mourning here.

**Ruth**    Hello?

*Pause.*

**Norman**    Hello?

*Pause.*

**Ruth**    Sorry?

*Pause.*

**Norman**    What for?

Who's that?

**Ruth**    Next door.

**Norman**    Next door? No one lives next door, they fucked off ages ago.

**Ruth**    Just moved in.

**Norman**    What do you want?

**Ruth**    Milk?

**Norman**    Milk?

**Ruth**    To borrow some milk, I can pay for it.

**Norman**    Milk?

**Ruth**    For my daughter, and to go with my tea.

**Norman**    There's a shop on the corner.

**Ruth**    It's closed.

**Norman**    Right. I'm a bit busy.

**Ruth**    Right.

I don't mean to be any trouble. I have money.

**Norman**    So?

**Ruth**    Sorry.

**Norman**    Aye, no bother.

**Norman** *pours himself a drink. There is another knock at the door.*

**Norman**    What fucking now?

**Ruth**    Hello?

**Norman**    Hello?

**Ruth**    Do you have any . . .

**Norman**    What?

**Ruth**    Milk. I have five pounds.

**Norman**    Can you not go to another shop?

**Ruth**    It's late, I have a daughter.

**Norman**    How does that stop you from going to the shop, lots of people have kids. They go to the shops. Send the kid to the shop, my mam always sent me to the shop.

**Ruth**    She's asleep.

**Norman**    She's dead.

**Ruth**    Sorry?

**Norman**   My mother is dead. Fifteen years now. She would send me for her fags.

**Ruth**   My daughter, she's asleep.

**Norman**   Send your man then.

**Ruth**   I don't have a man.

**Norman**   Your woman then.

**Ruth**   I am single.

**Norman**   None of my business.

**Ruth**   Just me and my daughter.

**Norman**   Take your daughter with you.

**Ruth**   I don't want to wake her.

**Norman**   Stick her in a pram.

**Ruth**   She's eight.

**Norman**   Probably too big for a pram.

**Ruth**   Yes.

**Norman**   Fuck's sake. Hang on.

**Norman** *stands and staggers to the fridge, he takes out a carton of milk and goes to the door. He opens the door and hands it through.*

**Norman**   There. Just leave me a bit for my coffee, alright. Just leave it by the door.

**Ruth**   Thank you.

**Norman**   Five pounds.

*Five pounds is handed through the door.*

**Norman** *stares at the hand for a second.*

**Ruth**   Thank you.

**Norman**   Aye.

**Norman** *closes the door. He returns to his chair and pours himself another drink. The cupboard door falls open and everything falls out.* **Norman** *calls out in frustration. He goes to put it all back with little success. There is another knock at the door.*

**Norman**    Fucking what now!!!

*The door slowly pushes open. A girl stands in the doorway. She steps forward.*

**Ruth**    Hello.

**Norman**    Excuse me. I'm in a towel here.

**Ruth**    Your milk is sour.

**Norman**    You can't just walk into a man's home.

**Ruth**    Your milk, it's gone sour.

**Norman**    What if I wasn't wearing a towel?

**Ruth**    Your milk.

**Norman**    So you keep saying.

**Ruth**    It's all lumps and I could smell it when you handed it to me.

**Norman**    I'll take it back then.

**Norman** *takes it back. Then doesn't know what to do with it.*

Suppose you will want your fiver back.

**Ruth**    Thank you.

**Norman**    Right, well, if you don't mind.

I'm mourning here, in my towel.

**Ruth**    I am sorry. My name is Ruth.

**Norman**    Mary.

**Ruth**    Ruth.

**Norman**    Mary lives downstairs. Ask her. She'll have some milk, give her a knock, she'll give you some milk.

**Ruth**    Mary. Thank you.

**Norman**    She'll chew your fucking ear off. Means well but she likes to know what's on the back end of every fart in this building.

**Ruth**    Thank you.

**Norman**    No bother. Close the door.

**Ruth**    Nice to meet you . . .

**Norman**    That's nice for you.

**Ruth**    Who were you talking with?

**Norman**    My dad. He wouldn't get in the cupboard.

**Ruth**    You keep your father in a cupboard?

**Norman**    Only when he's a naughty boy.

**Norman** *slams the door closed.* **Norman** *takes a drink and then forces everything back into the cupboard. He drags the suitcase back to the table.*

Right bastard, let's crack you open.

**Norman** *goes to the kitchen drawer and pulls out a large knife; he goes to the suitcase and begins to pick at the lock. There is a knock at the door,* **Norman***'s knife slips and he cuts his other hand deeply.* **Norman** *screams.*

*There is another knock at the door.*

**Ruth**    Hello?

**Norman**    What?

**Ruth**    Ruth?

**Norman**    What do you want?

**Ruth**    I've got milk.

**Norman**    Lovely.

**Ruth**    I got you milk.

**Norman**    Leave it by the door.

**Ruth**    Smells like there are cats out here.

**Norman**    Fuck the cats, there are no cats.

**Ruth**    The smell?

**Norman**    It's rain.

**Norman**'s *hand is bleeding heavily. He feels sick.*

Smelly fucking pissy rain. I don't feel good, I'm gonna . . .

**Norman** *dashes to the bathroom.*

*The door slowly opens and* **Ruth** *stands holding a small jug.*

**Ruth**    Hello?

The door opened. On its own.

Shall I leave leave the milk?

I'll just leave the milk on the side.

Are you alright?

**Ruth** *places the jug of milk on the bench. She looks around the bedsit.* **Ruth** *then goes across to the table. She sees the suitcase, the knife and a trail of blood from the table to the floor leading to the bathroom door. She walks to the door.*

*She listens at the door. She hears throwing up and moaning.*

Hello?

Blood, are you alright?

Do you need some help?

I can go and get your father?

**Ruth** *goes to the cupboard and opens it.*

**Norman** *opens the bathroom door.*

**Norman**    No!!!

**Ruth** *sees him stood with blood and sick all over. She screams.*

**Ruth**    Oh my god.

**Norman** *nearly faints and falls into* **Ruth***'s arms who immediately drops him.*

**Ruth**    Blood everywhere.

What have you done?

**Norman**    Nothing.

**Ruth**    You have killed you father?

**Norman**    No I haven't.

**Ruth**    You were shouting and cursing at him.

**Norman**    My dad's dead.

**Ruth**    You have killed him.

**Norman**    My dad's dead.

**Ruth**    Murdered.

**Norman**    No, my dad was dead before. I wasn't shouting at my dead dad, I was shouting at my dead dad's suitcase.

**Ruth**    Suitcase?

**Norman**    His suitcase.

It was his funeral today. They gave me the suitcase. All his belongings. I was trying to get it open.

**Ruth**    You have not killed your father?

**Norman**    Of course I haven't. Thought about it a couple of times.

**Ruth** *points to his hands.*

**Norman**    Cut me hand trying to open the fucking suitcase.

**Norman** *suddenly another gets a wave of dizziness and grabs* **Ruth** *for stability.*

**Ruth**    Sit, I will get you water.

**Norman**    I've got a drink.

*Gets his glass and refills it.*

**Ruth**    I think that might not be good for you.

**Norman**    It is, trust me.

*Gulps it down in one.*

**Norman**    Now, if you don't mind. It's been a very long day.

**Ruth**    We need to get you cleaned up and that hand bandaged.

**Norman**    I'll be fine.

**Ruth**    You're still losing blood.

**Norman**    Who are you?

**Ruth**    Ruth?

**Norman**    Next door. You wanted milk. You have a daughter.

**Ruth**    Her name is Wezo.

**Norman**    She's too big for her pram.

**Ruth**    Why you are wearing the shirt and tie?

**Norman** *laughs.*

**Ruth**    Do you have any bandaging?

**Norman**    Under the sink.

**Ruth**    I'm sorry about your father.

**Norman**    He was an arsehole.

**Ruth**    And that is his suitcase?

**Norman**    Aye.

**Ruth**    All that is left.

**Norman**    Aye.

**Ruth** *goes to have a look.*

**Ruth**    It's locked.

**Norman**    No shit, Sherlock.

**Ruth**    Key?

**Norman**    Combination.

**Ruth**    You know it?

**Norman**    That would be too easy with him.

**Ruth** *brings a bowl and bandages and sits at the table, she takes* **Norman**'s *hand.*

**Ruth**    This may hurt.

**Norman**    Fuck me, you fucking . . .

**Ruth**    Sorry.

**Norman**    Girl from the care home brought it to the funeral. Dad's wanted for me to have it apparently.

**Ruth**    What is inside?

**Norman**    Fuck knows.

**Ruth**    You must want to see if you're prepared to lose your fingers.

**Norman**    Fuck it. Just chuck it out.

**Ruth**    You should probably get those hands checked over by a doctor. This is just a patch up.

**Norman**    It'll be fine.

So you a nurse then?

**Ruth**    No.

**Norman**   You know what you're doing though.

**Ruth**   You pick things up. Being a mother helps.

**Norman**   Not from round here?

**Ruth**   No shit, Sherlock.

**Norman**   Where?

**Ruth**   Angola.

**Norman**   Nice?

**Ruth**   Nice?

**Norman**   Is it nice?

**Ruth**   It is beautiful, but not nice.

**Norman**   What do you mean?

**Ruth**   I should go. I have an early start tomorrow.

I am sure you will have work to go to.

**Norman**   Yeah, right.

**Ruth**   Sorry?

**Norman**   Don't be sorry. Not my fault.

**Ruth**   So hard to find work.

**Norman**   Too right. Fucking England? Fucking shithole. Government cutting off everything other than our heads. No jobs. Rich get richer, the poor get poorer. Hospitals are full. Sixteen fuckin hours I had to wait in casualty the other Saturday.

**Ruth**   You were sick?

**Norman**   Fell down the stairs.

**Ruth**   But you were seen?

**Norman**   Aye, after sixteen hours.

**Ruth**   But you were seen?

**Norman**    Eventually.

**Ruth**    Busy?

**Norman**    Fucking ridiculous, all the knackers were in.

**Ruth**    Must have been difficult.

**Norman**    Tell me about it, fucking disgrace.

**Ruth**    For the staff.

**Norman**    They get paid enough, don't you worry.

**Ruth**    Free health, free education. You are very fortunate.

**Norman**    Education. A fucking mess. Kids getting degrees if they can write their fucking name. Don't want to work though. Just want to be rich and famous dancing around on the Hickory Dickory Dock. Or they want to be gangsters.

**Ruth**    Wezo loves school so very much. She is a sponge to learning, and she has made many friends. I am so very happy to finally get her into a good school.

**Norman**    She will probably end up selling crack.

Hospitals are full, schools are full, no decent jobs going because the immigrants have taken them all.

**Ruth**    Immigrants?

**Norman**    Aye. Immigration. Sneaking in on boats 'illegally' in their fucking thousands and expecting us to give them homes, jobs or our benefits. Nowt left for the likes of me.

**Ruth**    Is that aimed at me?

**Norman**    I didn't say that.

**Ruth**    But I am an immigrant, I came to England by boat.

**Norman**    Yes, well.

**Ruth**    Well?

**Norman**    Well, I'm not talking about you, I'm talking about
. . .

**Ruth**    Yes?

**Norman**    The other lot.

**Ruth**    That doesn't even make sense. What other lot?

**Norman**    You know.

**Ruth**    No, I don't.

**Norman**    Oh, whatever.

**Ruth**    I want only to provide for my daughter and I will
work every hour of every day to do so.

**Norman**    Of course. Just trying to do your best, just like me.

But the government, the fucking government just want to
play games, always threatening. Threatening to sanction my
benefits. Put me on the streets. Sanction? Fuck all anyway.
Expected to live on what they give me.

**Norman** *pours himself a large drink.*

**Norman**    You working?

**Ruth**    I have five places I work.

**Norman**    Bit greedy, no wonder there's nothing left for the
rest of us.

**Ruth**    I am a cleaner.

**Norman**    Fuck that.

**Ruth**    Hardly enough to survive on what I earn.

**Norman**    Five jobs? Five?

**Ruth**    The cost to live.

**Norman**    Tell me about it. The cost of a drink these days.

**Ruth**    It is work and I am grateful.

**Norman**   You should say something.

**Ruth**   They have said if I am not happy I can leave and they will find someone else.

**Norman**   Arseholes. They will be making a fucking fortune off the backs of others.

**Ruth**   One day I will qualify.

**Norman**   Oh aye, what for?

**Ruth**   So, your father's suitcase?

**Norman**   Bugger it.

**Ruth**   May I look?

**Norman**   Why?

**Ruth**   Please?

**Norman**   If you like.

**Norman** *exits to the bedroom.* **Ruth** *walks around the table, closely looking at the case.*

**Ruth**   We must look at all options. Is the case itself valuable?

**Norman**   I doubt it.

**Ruth**   It looks very old.

**Norman**   He had it years, took it away with him all the time.

**Ruth**   Is it sentimental?

**Norman**   God, no.

**Ruth**   So all you want is what's inside, yes?

**Norman** *re-enters wearing a t-shirt and sweatpants, both look like they need a wash.*

**Norman**   Aye.

**Ruth** *grabs the kitchen knife from the table and raises it over her head.*

**Norman**   Jesus, what the fuck.

**Ruth** *slams the knife down into the suitcase and proceeds to cut the top off it.*

**Norman**   Why didn't I think of that?

**Ruth**   Options. You have to see things from all angles. May save your life one day.

**Ruth** *pulls opens the top of the case.*

**Norman**   Let the fucking dog see the fucking rabbit.

**Ruth**   Clothes.

**Norman**   Fucking knew it.

**Ruth**   Not good?

**Norman**   Apart from being completely out of date. My dad was three times my belly.

**Norman** *holds up a massive pair of trousers.*

**Ruth**   So?

**Norman**   Chuck the fucking lot.

**Norman** *throws the clothes onto the floor.*

**Ruth**   But they were your father's clothes.

**Norman**   So?

**Ruth** *searches through the case. She pulls out a large bright red striped suit. She looks confused.*

**Ruth**   Your father wore this?

**Norman** *bursts into laughter.*

**Norman**   Aye, weekends and summer holidays. Is the hat there?

**Ruth** *searches and pulls out a large striped hat.*

**Ruth**   Your father, what was he? A wizard.

**Norman** *puts the costume on.*

**Norman**   Ta-da. Meet the Professor.

**Ruth**   Professor?

**Norman**   That's what he called himself.

**Ruth**   Ah, so your father was a professor?

**Norman**   Was he fuck. He was a 'Punch and Judy' man.

**Ruth**   Punch and Judy?

**Norman**   Punch and Judy? Puppets? Not heard of it?

**Ruth**   No.

**Norman**   I suppose you wouldn't have, it's . . . very British.
There should be a bag?

**Ruth** *searches through the case until she finds the bag.*

**Ruth**   Here.

**Norman**   Have a look inside.

**Ruth**   What is it?

**Norman**   Go on.

**Ruth** *opens the bag; she suddenly jumps and drops the bag.*
**Norman** *laughs.*

**Ruth**   Monsters!!!

**Norman**   I know, fucking horrible, aren't they.

**Ruth**   What are they?

**Norman** *takes the bag and pours it open, half a dozen grotesque
puppets fall onto the floor.*

**Norman**   Meet the family.

**Norman**   Or should I say Dad's 'other' family.

**Ruth**   Family, they are puppets?

**Norman**   Yep, he cared more for them than he did us.

**Norman** *reaches into the pile and pulls out* **Mr Punch**.

**Norman**   Meet Punch. (*Breaks into* **Punch** *voice*.) Hello Ruth, give Punch a kiss.

**Norman** *pushes the doll towards* **Ruth**, *she backs away.*

**Norman** (*voice*)   Give Punch a kiss, or I'll smash your face.

**Ruth** *backs right away.*

**Ruth**   He's horrible.

**Norman**   Of course he is.

Let me see. Let's introduce you to Judy.

**Norman** *pulls* **Judy** *from the pile.*

**Norman**   Now everybody loved Judy. (*Voice*.) Hello dear, have you seen the sausages? I must find them for Mr Punch's tea or he will beat me with his stick, can you help me? Please?

**Norman** *reaches and pulls out a small* **Baby** *puppet.*

**Norman**   And this is Baby. Mr Punch has to look after Baby while Judy goes for the sausages. But Mr Punch fucks it up and Baby falls down the stairs.

**Norman** *drops the* **Baby** *back into the pile.*

**Norman**   Well, Judy comes home with the sausages, sees the Baby is hurt so calls the doctor. Punch attacks the doctor and then the policeman arrives and takes him off to jail.

**Ruth**   And the crocodile?

**Norman**   He eats the sausages.

**Ruth**   This is a children's story?

**Norman**   Oh, yes. Dad must have told that story a million times.

Every summer, come rain or shine. He travelled the world, well the seaside resorts of the north of England.

**Ruth**   And children wanted to see this?

**Norman**   Families would turn up in their thousands. They would laugh and cheer at the tale of domestic horror.

**Ruth**   Such a horrible story.

**Norman**   Yep. Guess it made people feel better about themselves.

Do you want a drink?

**Ruth**   No thank you.

**Norman**   That a religious thing is it?

**Ruth**   No.

**Norman**   It's a religious thing for me.

**Norman** *goes and pours himself another drink,* **Ruth** *continues to search through the case, she pulls out a box.*

**Ruth**   This?

**Norman**   A shoe box?

**Ruth** *takes the string from the box and opens the lid. She reads what is under the lid.*

**Ruth**   Property of George Gibson, Room seventeen. Elmgrove Care Community.

**Norman**   Couldn't look after himself in the end, went into a home.

**Ruth**   Did you not?

**Norman**   Fuck that.

**Ruth**   Full of things.

**Norman**   Any money in there?

**Ruth**   This?

**Norman**   His pipe.

**Ruth** *hands it to* **Norman**.

**Norman**   When I was a kid if I did anything wrong he would crack me on the top of the head with it. 'That's not how we do it', thought he was hilarious.

**Norman** *throws the pipe across the room.*

**Ruth**   What was your father like?

**Norman**   He was a bit like this nasty fucker really.

*Puts* **Mr Punch** *on his hand.*

**Norman**   That's not the way to do it.

**Norman** *bashes himself on his head with* **Mr Punch**'s *stick.*

**Ruth**   He would beat you?

**Norman**   Not really, most parents clipped their kids back into line when needs be. It was how it was done. Didn't do me any harm, did it?

**Norman** *goes cross-eyed.*

**Ruth**   He was a cruel man?

**Norman**   He had his . . . ways.

**Ruth**   Ways?

**Norman**   Aye, his way or the highway.

**Ruth**   And your mother?

**Norman**   Just like Judy. She was an angel and she was in fact called Judith.

**Ruth**   You were Baby?

**Norman**   Dad used to call the baby Norman.

**Ruth**   Family.

**Norman**   One little happy family.

In fact let me show you.

**Norman** *grabs the puppets and dives into the cupboard.*

Give me a minute.

*There are sounds of hammering, sawing and building.*

Ready?

**Ruth**    Yes.

**Norman**    Well open the fucking door then.

**Ruth** *opens the door revealing a fully built Punch and Judy tent.*

**Norman**    The Gibson's (*In the style of* The Simpsons.)

*This show should be frantic and chaotic from start to finish.*

*Curtain rises.*

**Punch**    Ladies and gentlemen, how do you do. If you all happy, me happy too. My name is Punch, the villain of the tale.

**Norman** *encourages audience to 'Cheer', 'Boo', 'Ahh' and join in when he thinks they should.*

**Judy**    Hello, boys and girls. My name is Judy.

And this is our beautiful son.

Our Norman.

**Punch**    Cost us fortune in milk and sausages, greedy little bu . . . baby.

**Judy**    Well, that's not very nice, is it boys and girls?

**Punch**    Not nice, but true.

**Judy**    Our beautiful little baby.

**Baby**    A popular boy, wouldn't say boo to a goose. Our little angel.

**Punch**    Spoiled by Judy.

**Baby**    A clever boy, top marks, school champion runner.

**Judy**   Won medals.

**Baby**   Could have trained for international, but someone had other ideas.

**Punch**   Couldn't afford that.

**Judy**   But could afford puppets for his show.

**Baby**   His 'silly silly' show.

**Punch**   To make money for the family.

**Judy**   Ran away to the coast most weekends and holidays.

**Baby**   With his other family.

**Punch**   Sometimes you would come.

**Judy**   Holidays at the seaside.

**Baby**   Yarmouth '76. Blackpool '78. Scarborough '80.

Can we have chips, Dad?

**Punch**   Too expensive. Drink your soup.

**Baby**   Buckets and spades?

**Punch**   Cheap and nasty. Use your hands.

**Baby**   Can we go on the donkey?

**Punch**   Riddled with fleas. They bite your fingers off.

**Judy**   The Punch and Judy Wars, always spying on the opposition.

**Baby**   Who were much funnier than him.

**Punch**   Gimmicky. No class. They won't last.

**Baby**   Thought I was the one with the dummy to spit out.

**Judy**   Baby growing up fast.

**Baby**   From one bottle to another.

**Punch**   Started dressing like a vampire.

*New* **Baby** *puppet. Young goth boy.*

**Baby**    My sixteenth birthday.

**Judy**    We threw you a party.

**Punch**    You were drunk.

**Baby**    Embarrassed me in front of my mates, in his fucking costume and hat.

**Punch**    Ungrateful little shit.

Ruined all your exams, didn't you, with all your fun and games.

**Judy**    Brought home by the police.

**Punch**    On many occasions.

**Judy**    Moved out for a while. Stayed with friends.

**Punch**    But soon came crawling back once they had enough.

**Baby**    Punch to the rescue.

**Punch**    Bring him into the family business.

**Judy**    Go on the road together.

**Punch**    Father and son.

**Baby**    The Professor and the student.

**Punch**    Ready to hand the hat over.

**Baby**    Ready to wear that cloak.

**Punch**    But you messed that up too.

**Baby**    Fucked that up too, didn't I.

**Punch**    That's not the way to do it.

**Judy**    Got a job.

**Punch**    Lost the job.

**Judy**    Got another job.

**Punch**    Lost the job.

**Judy**    Got another job.

**Punch**    Lost the job.

**Baby**    Alright!!! It's a tough world out there.

**Punch**    Couldn't get up on time, always calling in sick.

**Judy**    Met a girl. Fell in love.

**Baby**    Got engaged, moved in together.

**Punch**    Decided he loved drinking more, she soon left.

**Judy**    Missed my baby, worried a lot.

**Baby**    Missed Judy, she worried a lot.

**Punch**    Sneaked back when I was away. To be cleaned up, fed and given money.

**Judy**    My baby, Judy loves him.

**Baby**    And Baby loves Judy, too.

**Judy**    But sadly it wasn't to last.

**Baby**    Judy got poorly.

**Judy**    The doctor said nothing could be done.

**Punch**    Baby moved home, sorted himself out.

Put down his bottle.

**Punch** *and* **Baby**    And we all looked after Judy.

**Judy**    Judy died and went to heaven.

**Punch** *and* **Baby**    Broke our hearts.

**Punch**    Baby went back to the bottle, and fighting and stealing.

Stealing from Punch.

**Baby**   Punch shouted at Baby.

**Punch**   Baby punched Punch.

**Baby**   Punch threw Baby onto the streets.

**Punch**   Baby gave me no choice.

**Baby**   Baby was your baby.

**Punch**   Baby broke Punch's heart.

**Baby**   Punch was hit by a car on the front at Whitley Bay.

**Punch**   Both hips shattered. Baby could have looked after me.

**Baby**   Fuck that. Care home for Punch.

**Punch**   No time for Mr Punch.

**Baby**   That's right.

**Punch**   Too busy for dear old Punch.

**Baby**   That's right.

**Punch**   Punch and Judy's house was sold.

**Baby**   Mostly for Punch's care home.

**Punch**   Baby got a chunk and drank it away.

Propping up bars in pubs and clubs.

Everyone's friend to begin with.

The living legend. Everyone knows his name.

But as the money went, so did the 'friends'.

Drinking from cans and bottles in his shitty hovel or on the streets.

Sleeping, pissing, shitting in corners.

Now a centre of gossip and humiliation. Everyone knows his name.

Waking most mornings dressed in his own filth. Body and brain twisting in pain.

Got to feed it make the pain go away, go away.

All gone away. Job. Family. Respect.

**Baby**    Punch died and went to hell.

**Punch**    Baby's all alone.

That's the way to do it.

That's the way to do it.

That's the way to do it.

**Baby**    SHUT UP!!!

*Puppets fight.*

*Curtain drops and cupboard door slams shut. We can hear sobbing coming from the cupboard.*

**Ruth** *sits in silence for a short time.*

**Ruth**    Alright in there?

**Norman**    You can go now, the show's over.

**Ruth**    I shouldn't leave you.

**Norman**    Get back to your own family.

Go on, fuck off.

**Ruth** *goes to leave.*

**Norman** *thinks* **Ruth** *has gone and creeps from the cupboard. Takes a seat and a drink.*

*She stands and watches him for a while.*

**Norman** *reaches for the shoe box and begins to look through it.*

**Norman** *brings out photographs and items all relating to a family, especially* **Norman**.

*Memories.*

**Norman** *becomes emotional again.*

**Ruth**    I think your father really loved you.

**Norman**    What the fuck are you still doing here?

**Ruth**    The box was important.

**Norman**    A sad little life in a sad little shoe box.

**Ruth**    Not his life, yours.

**Norman**    Trinkets of shit memories.

**Ruth**    Not to him.

**Norman**    The show? You heard what he said.

**Ruth**    Your words.

**Norman**    Look, will you please leave me alone. No one asked you to be here.

**Ruth**    I am worried about you, Norman.

**Norman**    Well, don't be.

**Ruth**    You shouldn't be on your own.

**Norman**    I've been on my own most of my life.

**Ruth**    Not true, I'm sure.

**Ruth**    What would you know? What would you know about my life? You don't know about me. You haven't a clue about me.

**Ruth**    I can see you are sad.

**Norman**    Am I?

**Ruth**    And that is fine. You're sad because your father has passed.

**Norman**    Couldn't give a shit. He didn't care about me.

**Ruth**    You are not being truthful.

**Norman**    Truthful?

**Ruth**    Look at the box. He wanted to pass it on.

**Norman**    Fuck the box.

I'm not sad, I'm not fucking sad.

**Ruth**    You need to grieve. That's how you move on.

**Norman**    Grieve? Fuck off. Hadn't seen him in years.

**Ruth**    And he is gone now and I am sure you will feel some guilt for not seeing him.

**Norman**    Guilt? Get the fuck out, now!!!

**Ruth**    Let me explain.

**Norman**    Go on. Get out.

**Ruth**    Please, listen to me.

**Norman**    Will you just fuck off out of my life.

Just fuck off back to wherever you fucking came from.

*An awkward silence you could park a bus in.* **Norman** *throws the shoe box back into the case. He pours himself another drink and goes to the door and opens it as an indication for* **Ruth** *to go. She goes to leave then stops herself turning to* **Norman**.

**Ruth**    Why would you say that?

**Norman**    What?

**Ruth**    Back where I came from?

**Norman**    What?

**Ruth**    I am only trying to help you.

**Norman**    No one asked you to.

**Ruth**    We are neighbours.

**Norman**    So what?

**Ruth**    That means something surely?

**Norman**    Fuck all.

**Ruth**    I will go then.

**Norman**    Right.

**Ruth** Sorry to have . . .

**Norman** Right.

**Ruth** *goes to leave and stops herself. She turns looks at* **Norman** *with anger, but then composes herself and leaves.*

**Norman** What???

**Ruth** Nothing.

**Ruth** *exits.*

**Norman** *pours himself a large drink.*

**Norman** Coming into my home.

Not even invited.

**Norman** *slugs the drink down.*

Don't need no one's help.

Don't need no one.

**Norman** *pours hinself another large drink and slugs it down.*
**Norman** *takes the suitcase and all its contents and throws it into a cupboard.*

Don't need no one.

**Norman** *puts on some music and sits.*

Don't need no one.

**Norman** *drinks from the bottle.*

Well done, dick-head.

That's the way to do it.

That's the way to do it.

That's the way to do it.

*Lights down.*

*End of Act One.*

## Act Two

## Ruth

*Music.*

*Lights up.*

**Norman** *is asleep in a chair. He is wearing different clothes indicating a change in time but not his situation. He is surrounded by bottles, cans and random items showing druken behaviour. (Traffic cones, mannequin dummy, etc.) Loud music is playing.* **Norman** *has a black eye.*

*There is a loud banging on the door.*

**Ruth**   Norman?

Norman?

Norman, please!!!

**Norman** *awakes from his deep slumber.*

**Norman**   What the fuck?

*The banging and shouting continue and intensify.*

**Norman** *turns off music.*

Alright.

**Norman** *opens the door to* **Ruth**.

**Norman**   Where's the fucking fire?

**Ruth**   Please, Norman, I need your help.

**Norman**   Have those smack-rats broken in again. Wait there.

**Norman** *goes to the cupboard and brings out a baseball bat.*

Right, I'll sort these bastards out.

**Ruth**   It's Wezo.

**Norman**   Where is she?

**Ruth**   Having her breakfast.

**Norman**   With the smack-rats.

**Ruth**   What smack-rats?

**Norman**   What's going on here?

**Ruth**   I need your help.

**Norman**   You woke me up?

**Ruth**   My daughter.

**Norman**   What about her?

**Ruth**   I need you to look after her.

**Norman**   Look after her?

**Ruth**   I have to work.

**Norman**   And this has what to do with me?

**Ruth**   I have no one.

**Norman**   Is she not at school?

**Ruth**   Teachers' strike.

**Norman**   Strike? Teachers? Fuck me. They get paid a fucking fortune, finish at three. Shit-loads of holidays. What they got to fucking strike about.

**Ruth**   Can you help me, please?

**Norman**   Me? I don't think so.

**Ruth**   Please? I must work. I cannot lose my work.

**Norman**   Just tell them you are sick.

**Ruth**   They do not care. They will just replace me.

**Norman**   They can't do that.

**Ruth**   Yes, they can.

Can you help me, please?

**Norman**    Sorry, not my circus, not my elephants.

**Ruth**    Please? If I lose my work I lose our home.

**Norman**    Sorry but no.

**Ruth**    Please, Norman. I have no one else.

**Norman**    No, thank you . . . ask Mary.

**Ruth**    She's visiting her sister.

**Norman**    Her sister's dead.

**Ruth**    She said. That is why I have no choice but to ask you.

**Norman**    That's nice of you.

**Ruth**    I beg you, please.

**Norman**    No, thank you.

**Norman** *goes to close the door.* **Ruth** *drops to the floor and begins to beg.*

**Ruth**    Please, please . . .

**Norman** *closes the door and goes to open a can of beer.*

*The audience should really hate* **Norman** *for a moment.*

**Norman** *puts down the can and goes back to the door and opens it.*

**Norman**    How long?

**Ruth**    You will help me?

**Norman**    How long?

**Ruth**    I would be finished at three.

**Norman**    That's six frigging hours.

**Ruth**    She has much school work to do. She has her lunch. She has everything she needs. I have to go, I am so late. Thank you, Norman, thank you so very much.

**Norman**    Alright, fine.

**Ruth**   And you will not drink?

**Norman**   What?

**Ruth**   I need you not to drink. Not around my daughter. Can you do that?

**Norman**   Aye.

I'm not a fucking alchy you know.

**Ruth** *looks around the destruction in the room.*

**Ruth**   I have told Wezo you will be looking after her. She is excited to meet you.

**Norman**   How did you know I would say yes?

**Ruth**   Because behind those red eyes is kindness.

**Norman**   Is that a compliment?

**Ruth**   Yes.

**Ruth** *kisses* **Norman** *on the cheek.*

**Ruth**   You need to shower. I must go. Thank you so much, Norman.

**Ruth** *exits.*

**Norman**   Fuck!!!

**Norman** *goes back to the can. He stares at the can, then the door, then the can, then the door.*

**Norman**   Fuck!!!

**Norman** *paces back and forth then exits into the bathroom. We hear a shower.*

*Lights down.*

*Spotlight up on* **Ruth** *in blank space. She is wearing cleaner's uniform and holding a mop.*

*This section shows no location and conversations are spoken in the direction of the audience.*

**Ruth**    I am so very sorry I am late.

I can explain, I had to find someone to look after my daughter.

Her school is closed, I am really sorry about being late.

Please, you can't, what I get already is not enough.

I am sorry, I didn't mean to talk to you like that.

*Spotlight down on* **Ruth**. *Spotlight up on* **Norman**.

**Norman**    Hello.

It's Wezo, isn't it?

My name is Norman, I live next door.

Your mam said for me to sit with you.

I'll be back in a minute.

*Spotlight down on* **Norman**, *we hear* **Norman** *throw up*.

*Spotlight up on* **Ruth**.

**Ruth**    I promise it will never happen again.

I have never been late before today.

I cannot stay any longer today, I have other work to get to.

I will do anything you want but please, I cannot.

If you do that I will lose my home.

*Spotlight down on* **Ruth**. *Spotlight up on* **Norman**.

**Norman**    So your mam says you have homework?

Well, maybe I can help you with it?

Industrial Revolution?

Maybe not then.

Where's your telly?

You don't have a telly.

*Spotlight down on* **Norman**. *Spotlight up on* **Ruth**.

**Ruth**   I am sorry. My other employer made me stay overtime.

I understand this is not your problem.

I see. I have bills I have to pay.

I cannot not have a roof over her head. I promise it will not happen again.

I can work this weekend. To compensate my lateness.

There is no need to find anyone else.

I am a good worker.

*Spotlight down on* **Ruth**. *Spotlight up on* **Norman**.

**Norman**   What's that you're eating?

No thanks.

You got anything else?

Got any crisps?

I haven't eaten fruit in years.

*Spotlight down on* **Norman**. *Spotlight up on* **Ruth**.

**Ruth**   I was at the bathroom.

I was only gone five minutes.

I haven't had another break today.

I understand.

Thousands begging to do this work.

You want me to make note of all toilet breaks.

And that comes off my time?

I understand.

*Spotlight down on* **Ruth**. *Spotlight up on* **Norman**.

**Norman**    And the farmer says you turn the handle and I'll hold the bucket.

**Norman** *finds that very funny.*

You're bored?

Aye, I'm bored.

You got any playing cards?

Do you know pontoon?

You got any money?

You could have a sleep?

I could have a sleep.

I don't know.

Hang on, maybe I do.

Don't move a muscle.

I'll be right back.

*Spotlight down on* **Norman**. *Spotlight up on* **Ruth**. *She is sobbing. She is tired and she is stressed to breaking point.*

**Ruth**    I am fine.

It has been a long day.

For my daughter, her name is Wezo.

Wezo.

Wezo.

Yes, I love her very much.

She is waiting at home.

My neighbour Norman is looking after her.

**Ruth** *breaks down again and sobs.*

*Spotlight down on* **Ruth***. Spotlight up on* **Norman** *now dressed in his dad's puppet costume.*

**Norman**    Hello, Wezo, my name's Professor Norman.

This is Mr Punch. Say hello, Mr Punch.

**Punch**    Hello, Wezo.

And this is Judy. Say hello, Judy.

**Judy**    Hello, Wezo.

**Norman**    Hold onto your socks, Wezo.

For do we have a show for you?

**Punch**    No we do not.

**Norman**    Shut your face, Mr Punch. Wish me luck, Judy.

**Judy**    Good luck, Norman.

**Norman**    Here we go.

**Norman** *takes in a deep breath. Spotlight down.*

*Return to the bedsit.*

**Norman** *opens the door dressed as The Professor. He looks exhausted.*

Thank you.

**Norman** *closes the door and takes a deep breath. He spies the can of lager and heads towards it holding it like a holy grail.*

**Norman** *sings 'You Are So Beautiful' then cracks the can and drinks it down in one. He sits on the chair and begins to pull out the puppets, looking at them carefully.*

**Punch**    Well?

**Judy**    Well?

**Norman**    We did OK?

**Punch**    That's the way to do it.

**Judy**    I think she liked us.

It was good to be back.

**Punch**    That's the way to do it.

**Norman**    She was OK.

**Judy**    You haven't had a drink all day.

**Norman**    No, I haven't.

**Punch**    That's the way to do it.

**Judy**    We are very proud of you.

**Punch**    That's the way to do it.

**Norman**    Never a straight answer from Mr Punch.

**Mr Punch** *bops* **Norman** *on the head at the same time as a knock on the door.*

**Ruth**    Norman.

**Norman**    I didn't eat them.

**Ruth** *opens the door.*

**Ruth**    May I come in?

**Norman**    If you must.

**Ruth**    I do not wish to impose any further on your day.

**Norman**    Behave yourself, come in. How's the bairn?

**Ruth**    Bairn?

**Norman**    Wezo?

**Ruth**    Wezo is asleep. She sings that she had a great time with you, Norman.

**Norman**    Really?

**Ruth**    That she got to hear your jokes, play cards and meet Mr Punch and Judy.

**Norman**    They had a good time too, didn't you.

**Punch**    That's the way to do it.

**Judy**    A very polite young lady.

**Ruth**    She said she felt very special.

**Norman**    Good.

**Ruth**    She asks when you can come again.

**Ruth** *brings out ten pounds and hands it to* **Norman**.

**Norman**    What's that?

**Ruth**    For you?

**Norman**    What for?

**Ruth**    For today.

**Norman**    Fuck off.

I don't want your money.

**Ruth**    But you allowed me to work.

**Norman**    Buy me a beer sometime.

**Norman** *goes to the fridge and takes a can.*

**Ruth**    Do you have one I could have?

**Norman**    Thought you didn't drink.

**Ruth**    Today has been . . . difficult.

**Norman** *throws* **Ruth** *a can.*

**Norman**    Only one mind. I've only got six.

*They crack their cans together.*

**Norman**    Down your neck.

**Ruth**    Saúde.

**Norman**    What's that?

**Ruth**    It's Portugese?

**Norman**    Saúde.

**Norman** *repeats then downs his can and emits a huge burp.*

**Ruth** *takes a huge gulp then also emits a burp. They both find this very funny and continue to outdo each other.*

**Norman**    Your boss give you a hard time then?

**Ruth**    She made many threats.

**Norman**    Threatened you?

**Ruth**    My job.

**Norman**    You should have told her to fuck off.

**Ruth**    Then I would have no work.

**Norman**    You not have rights?

**Ruth**    Not till I get citizenship.

**Norman**    Citizenship?

**Ruth**    To become a citizen of England.

**Norman**    Why you would want to be part of this shithole.

**Ruth**    It is my home.

**Norman**    Home? A shitty room you have to work your fingers to the bone to pay for.

**Ruth**    I must tell you about where I came from to live in my shitty room with working five jobs cleaning corridors and toilets in offices and stores.

There was once a young girl who lived in a beautiful place with her beautiful family. But a cruel government took their voices, saying if the people spoke out about the people in power, they would stamp their feet.

The girl was fourteen years old and a decision was made for her to marry a rich and powerful man old enough to be her grandfather. If my parents refused they would be imprisoned or even killed.

Her mother stole her from her beautiful home and family into a thousand miles of desert where they avoided soldiers and savage dogs both who would tear them apart for sport.

To a border far away and to pay all her money and jewellery in gold to a man with a boat set for Europe.

Saying goodbye to her mother who she would not see again.

Pushed onto a ship not fit enough to hold water never mind a hundred souls.

To Italy and the streets begging for food and water. Being chased and spat at by children.

Given a room from hell by a cruel man meaning to cause her harm. One night he gave her a child she didn't ask for.

Escaping that place, from Italy into France where she meets different beautiful family from different beautiful country now in rubble from civil war and also on a journey of survival. They take her unto them and to a northern coastal town where yet another wealthy man is paid to take them to England.

Another broken boat, that only makes it half way before hitting a storm and filling with water. Only the girl and the captain are pulled from the water, the beautiful family's journey ended there.

Taken into England and a system so complex and terrifying where strangers smile, tell them it will be alright yet they know they will probably be sent home to their death.

Her home was a cell with a bed and a toilet until after months she is taken into care because she is only fourteen years old.

**Norman**    That a fairy tale?

**Ruth**    No, an honest truth.

**Norman**    And the girl?

**Ruth**    Snuck into England on a boat and years later rents a shitty room with her eight-year-old daughter Wezo, next door to a funny man called Norman.

*They both sit in silence for a while.*

**Norman**    I don't know what to say.

**Ruth**    Say nothing, just understand.

**Norman**    I meant your room, you know?

**Ruth**    What?

**Norman**    Go back to where you came from, I meant your room.

**Ruth**    I see.

**Norman**    I was angry.

**Ruth**    Some people in England look at me and make an assumption of who I am. They hear my accent and pull a face. When I try to tell them my name, they get it wrong. My real name is not Ruth, my name is 'Rute', but it is easier for me to be called Ruth. Not for me but them. People think I am here to take. I want nothing but a safe home for my family. But people think I will take what they think they are due. I want to work and all the work I do is the work that those people will not do. You call me greedy for wanting to work.

**Norman**    I didn't mean it.

**Ruth**    You said it.

**Norman**    I say a lot of shit, and it is just shit. Don't mean anything by it.

**Ruth**    Why say it?

**Norman**    I don't know.

But I am not a racist.

**Ruth**    No, you hate everyone.

**Norman**   I am sorry.

**Ruth**   I think you are not a happy man?

**Norman**   No, but who is?

**Ruth**   I am, most of the time.

**Norman**   How do you cope?

**Ruth**   Because I do. My room is my home, which I can now pay for and feed us. I am thankful for that.

**Norman**   That is where you come from?

**Ruth**   Exactly. Every day is a great adventure.

**Norman**   Not for me it's not.

**Ruth**   It could be.

**Norman**   Nah, my map's mapped.

**Ruth**   Un-map it then.

**Norman**   Not that easy, is it.

**Ruth**   No, it's not.

**Norman**   I miss my family.

**Ruth**   I miss mine.

**Norman**   Why are you doing this?

**Ruth**   What?

**Norman**   Even talking to me.

**Ruth**   We are neighbours.

**Norman**   And?

**Ruth**   We look after each other?

**Norman**   Not really, not 'til now.

**Ruth**   I think it's important.

**Norman**   You don't have to.

**Ruth**    I know.

**Norman**    I can look after myself.

**Ruth**    I can see that.

*They both laugh.* **Norman** *pours a drink. Looks at it and sighs.*

**Ruth**    Don't drink it then.

**Norman**    I want to.

**Ruth**    Then why sigh?

**Norman** *looks at it and then drinks it and then regrets.*

**Norman**    Takes away the pain.

**Ruth**    Delays, not take away.

You need to face pain for it to go away.

**Norman**    Just want to feel better.

**Ruth**    You will.

**Ruth**    Wait there.

**Ruth** *dashes from the room, leaving* **Norman**. *She soon returns.*

*She carries a CD which she puts into the player. Music plays and* **Ruth** *begins to dance.*

**Ruth**    Dance.

**Norman**    Fuck off.

**Ruth**    Dance the anger out.

**Norman**    No.

**Ruth**    Dance, Norman!

**Norman** *slowly begins to dance and really gets into it. The music builds as does the dancing. They both fall into the chairs exhausted.* **Norman** *is smiling.*

**Ruth**    You are smiling.

**Norman**    Maybe.

**Ruth**    No maybe.

**Norman**    Are you an angel?

**Ruth**    No?

**Norman**    I think you are.

**Ruth**    I should go back to where I come from.

**Norman**    Are you taking the piss?

**Ruth**    Yes.

**Norman**    I am sorry.

**Ruth**    I know.

**Norman**    Thank you.

**Ruth**    What for?

**Norman**    Giving a shit.

**Ruth**    Giving a shit?

**Norman**    Caring.

**Ruth**    You are welcome, now I must get back.

**Norman**    For Wezo.

**Ruth**    You will see her again tomorrow.

**Norman**    Will I?

**Ruth**    Yes. We shall go for coffee and cake.

**Norman**    You're taking me for coffee and cake?

**Ruth**    Yes.

You are tired.

**Norman**    Like you wouldn't believe. I would give anything for a good night's sleep.

**Ruth**    Then sleep.

**Ruth** *begins to sing. She walks to* **Norman** *and puts her hand on his head.*

**Ruth**    Sleep.

**Norman** *is asleep.* **Ruth** *continues to sing as she walks to the door and turns to a sleeping* **Norman***.*

**Ruth**    Goodnight, Mr Punch. Tomorrow is another day.

**Ruth** *exits into a brighter light.*

*Music.*

*The end.*